Walk

Military Base

Peggy Pancella

Heinemann Library
Chicago, Illinois

Customer Service   888–454–2279

Visit our website at www.heinemannlibrary.com

Photo research by Jill Birschbach
Designed by Joanna Hinton-Malivoire and Q2A Creative
Printed in China by South China Printing Co.

10 09 08 07 06
10 9 8 7 6 5 4 3 2 1

Library of Congress Cataloging-in-Publication Data
Pancella, Peggy.
  Military base / Peggy Pancella.-- 1st ed.
     p. cm. -- (Neighborhood walk)
  Includes bibliographical references and index.
  ISBN 1-4034-6217-8 (hc) -- ISBN 1-4034-6223-2 (pb)
  1. Military bases--Juvenile literature. 2. City and town life--Juvenile
literature. I. Title. II. Series.
  UC400.P36 2005
  355.7--dc22
                          2005010759

Acknowledgments
The author and publisher are grateful to the following for permission to reproduce copyright material: U.S. Air Force pp. 6 (Master Sgt. Jim Varhegyi), 27 (Staff Sgt. Randy Redman): U.S. Marines 4 (Sgt. Luis R. Agostini), 8 (Sgt. Joshua S. Higgins), 9 (Cpl. Ryan S. Scranton), 10 (Lance Cpl. Patrick J. Floto), 13 (Lance Cpl. Rose A. Muth), 20 (LCpl. Michael I. Gonzalez), 22 (Cpl. Jennifer Brofer), 23 (Cpl. Kurt Fredrickson), 26 (Cpl. Trevor M. Carlee): U.S. Navy 5 (Chief Photographer's Mate Spike Call), 7 (Patrick Nichols), 11 (Photographer's Mate 1st Class Marvin Harris), 12 (Photographer's Mate 2nd Class Richard J. Brunson), 14 (Photographer's Mate 2nd Class Michael Larson), 15 (Cryptologic Technician 1st Class Patrick D. Wormsley), 16 (Photographer's Mate 1st Class William R. Goodwin), 17 (Photographer's Mate 1st Class William R. Goodwin), 18 (Photographer's Mate 1st Class William R. Goodwin), 19 (Chief Journalist James H. Junior), 21 (Photographer's Mate 3rd Class Chris Weibull), 24 (Photographer's Mate Airman Joan Kretschmer), 25 (Photographer's Mate 2nd Class Aaron Peterson), 28 (Chief Photographer's Mate Johnny Bivera), 29 (Photographer's Mate 1st Class Michael A. Worner).

Cover photograph reproduced with the permission of Accentalaska.com (Ken Graham)

Some words are shown in bold, **like this**. You can find out what they mean by looking in the glossary.

Contents

Let's Visit a Military Base

Guards check everyone who enters and leaves a military base.

People everywhere live in **neighborhoods**. A neighborhood is a small part of a larger **community**, such as a city or town. A neighborhood's people and places help to make it special.

Some neighborhoods are **military bases**. Members of the **armed forces** live, work, and **train** here. A base may have hundreds or thousands of people. Many bases are near towns or small cities.

Bases may be in the United States or in other countries.

Homes

There are many different kinds of homes on **military bases**. Many **military** families live in houses. Others live in apartments. Some homes have yards where people can play and relax.

Homes on military bases may be large or small.

Bachelor Housing
WELCOME CENTER

Some barracks are like large apartment buildings.

Some people live in **barracks**. Barracks are buildings where members of the military live together. These people often do not have families living on the base. There are usually separate barracks for men and women.

7

Getting Around

Some military workers live in town and drive to the base each day.

On **military bases**, many people use cars or buses to get from place to place. Some walk or ride bikes near their homes. People drive cars or ride buses when they need to go into town.

Military workers sometimes get around in special ways. They may line up in groups and march together. They may ride in special vehicles such as planes, jeeps, or tanks. Some use boats at bases that are near water.

Jeeps and other military vehicles do special jobs.

Schools

Many **military bases** have their own schools. These schools may be large or small. Children from the base can sometimes walk to school. They may ride bikes or buses, too.

Many base schools have outdoor play areas.

These students listen to a story.

Some **military** children go to school in town. Children on bases in other countries may hear different languages at these town schools. They can understand more at the base school, where the teachers speak English.

Working

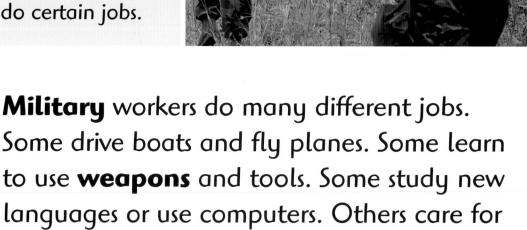

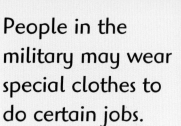

People in the military may wear special clothes to do certain jobs.

Military workers do many different jobs. Some drive boats and fly planes. Some learn to use **weapons** and tools. Some study new languages or use computers. Others care for people who need help.

Many workers help the **military base** run
smoothly. Some build houses and other
buildings. Some make and repair vehicles and
other equipment. Others work at stores,
restaurants, and other businesses on the base.

A base may have
different kinds
of businesses.

Keeping Safe

Many workers help keep a **military base** safe. Special **military** police officers guard the base. Sometimes they **patrol** the base on foot. They may also ride on bikes or in cars.

Military police are ready to help when problems happen.

Firefighters need special training and equipment to keep everyone safe.

Many bases also have firefighters and **emergency** workers. They rush to help when people are hurt, sick, or in danger. Their quick work can save people's lives.

15

Shopping

Military bases have different kinds of places to shop. A **commissary** is like a grocery store. A **post exchange (PX)** or **base exchange (BX)** sells uniforms, supplies, and other special equipment. There may be other shops as well.

Sometimes many stores share one building.

Sometimes **military** families go into town to shop. Stores in town sell different kinds of products. Many towns near bases have large shopping centers called **malls**.

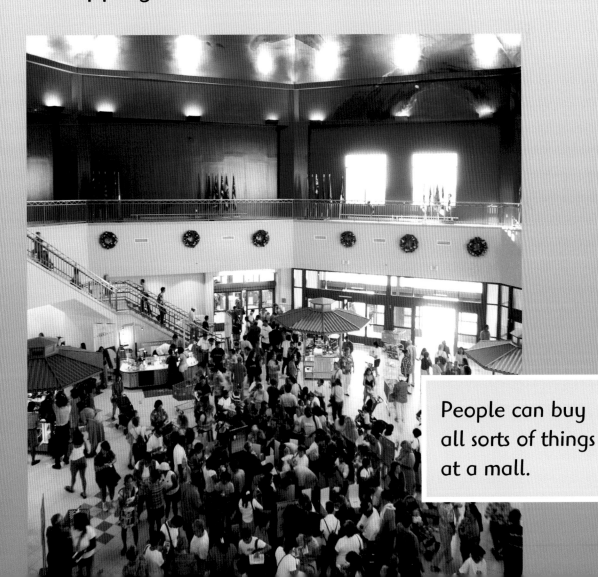

People can buy all sorts of things at a mall.

Food

Families often get much of their food from the **military base's commissary**. They can buy many different kinds of groceries there. Towns near military bases have grocery stores and other food shops, too.

A commissary sells different kinds of groceries.

Some bases have cafeterias where people can get food quickly.

There are lots of places for **military** families to eat as well. Most bases have one or more restaurants. Some sell fast food and others serve sit-down meals. Nearby towns may have restaurants, too.

Libraries

Many **military bases** have libraries. People can borrow books and magazines to read. There may be videos and other materials as well.

Some base libraries are large and others are small.

Computers may
be used for work
or play.

People can use computers to look up
information that they need. Sometimes they
can play computer games, too. People may
also join book clubs, see special shows, or do
other activities at base libraries.

Money and Mail

Banks may **lend** people money for the things they need.

A **military base** usually has at least one bank to handle people's money. People often do business inside the bank. Some banks may have drive-up windows or **ATMs**.

Most bases have post offices, too. People can mail letters or packages from there. Sometimes they can pick up their mail at the post office. Sometimes letter carriers deliver the mail to people's homes.

People can send packages to anywhere in the world.

Other Places on a Military Base

Military bases need many different kinds of buildings. Some buildings have offices or classrooms. Bases often have at least one place of worship.

Many different religious services may be held at a military base.

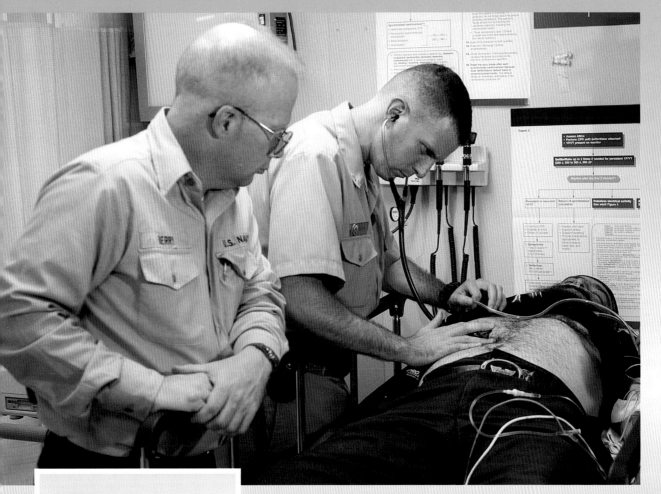

Military doctors treat all kinds of health problems.

Military bases also have doctors' offices. Sometimes they have hospitals, too. People can get care here when they are sick or hurt.

25

Having Fun

Military bases often have their own sports teams.

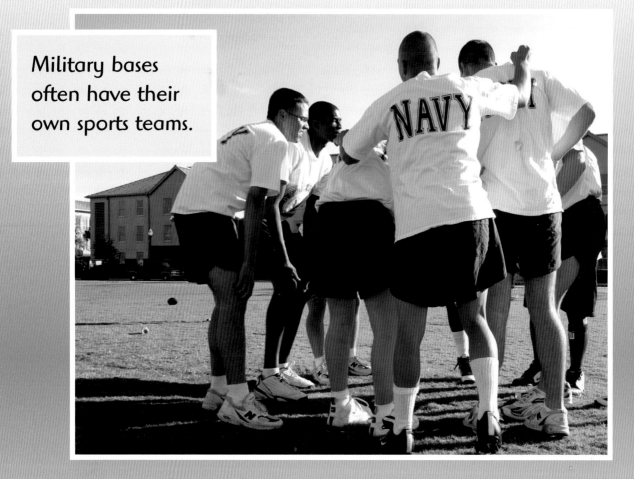

Many **military** families like to play or relax in their own yards. Some **military bases** have ball fields and other play areas. Bases may also have movie theaters or concert halls where singers and bands perform.

Many bases have **fitness centers** with gyms and exercise machines. People can also play in games rooms and do other activities. Some bases have **museums** that tell about history. People can go into town for other activities, too.

People do many kinds of exercises at the gym.

The Military Base Comes Together

People on **military bases** often work together. They collect food, clothing, and other items for those in need. They raise money to help others. They send letters and packages to military workers around the world.

People send important supplies to **military** workers.

These people have just finished their military training.

People on bases may have parties and other fun events, too. Sometimes there are parades and **ceremonies** on special days. People also share food, music, games, and fun. All these things make military bases great places to live.

Glossary

armed forces groups that protect a country on land, air, and sea

ATM bank machine that people use to put in and take out money

barracks building or group of buildings where military people may live together

base exchange (BX) store on a military base that sells different kinds of items

ceremony formal event that includes actions done in a special, important way

commissary store on a military base that sells groceries

community group of people who live in one area, or the area where they live

emergency sudden event that makes you act quickly

fitness center building with places and equipment where people can exercise

lend allow somebody to use something for a period of time

mall shopping center with many different kinds of stores in one building

military having to do with the armed forces

military base protected area where members of the armed forces live, work, and train

museum   place where special or important items are shown

neighborhood   small area of a city or town

patrol   travel through an area to keep it safe

post exchange (PX)   store on a military base that sells many kinds of items

train   learn and practice certain actions

weapon   object that can be used in fighting

More Books to Read

Easter, Julie W. *My Military Dad*. Pittsburgh: Dorrance Publishing, 2004.
An older reader can help you with this book.

Ferguson-Cohen, Michelle. *Daddy, You're My Hero!* Brooklyn: Little Redhaired Girl Publishing, 2003.

Ferguson-Cohen, Michelle. *Mommy, You're My Hero!* Brooklyn: Little Redhaired Girl Publishing, 2003.

Kehoe, Stasia Ward. *I Live at a Military Post*. New York: PowerKids Press, 1999.

Korman, Lewis J., and Matthew Naythons. *A Day in the Life of the United States Armed Forces*. New York: HarperCollins, 2003.
An older reader can help you with this book.

Index

9/14 ⑧